Listen Up Now:
How to increase growth and profit by really listening to your customers and clients

By

Dr Darryl Cross

Published by Crossways Publishing

ISBN-10: 0-9806101-5-X

ISBN-13: 978-0-9806101-5-4

Books by Dr Darryl Cross

Hard copy or Kindle versions are available at
www.amazon.com

Audio versions are available at www.DrDarryl.com

Growing up Children: How To Get 5-12 Year Olds To Behave & Do As They're Told

Teenager Trouble-shooting: How to Stop Your Adolescent Driving You Crazy

The Dark Clouds at Work: How to Manage Depressed Staff in the Workplace Whilst Increasing Morale and Productivity

Stopping Your Self-sabotage: Steps to Increase Self-confidence

In Pursuit of Success and Happiness: A Practical Guide

CONTENTS

Page

CHAPT 1: FIRST THINGS FIRST　　7
First Things First　　9
1. First Impressions　　11
2. Interpersonal Skills　　12
3. Body Language　　14
4. Verbal & Non-Verbal Communication　　15
Summary　　21

CHAPT 2: THE ART OF COMMUNICATION　　23
The Basics of Communication　　25
Summary　　29

CHAPTER 3: LISTENING IN BUSINESS　　31
Two Main Myths　　32
Training Practices　　35
The Consultant Listener　　37
Summary　　42

CHAPT 4: WHAT IS IT & WHAT IS IT NOT?　　45
Why Don't We Listen?　　45
Listening Bad Habits　　51
What is Listening?　　53
What it is Not　　54
What it is　　55
Summary　　58

CHAPT 5: WHAT ARE THE SKILLS?   61
The Levels of Listening   61
The Skills of Listening   62
Summary   71

CHAPT 6: ASKING POWERFUL
QUESTIONS?   73
The Power is in the Question   73
Problem Questions   75
Effective Questions   80
Summary   86

CHAPT 7: THE KNOWING DOING GAP   89
Increase all the Bottom Lines   89
Overcoming the Barriers   91
Summary   94

APPENDICES   95
ABOUT THE AUTHOR   117

CHAPTER 1:

FIRST THINGS FIRST

Listening. We all think that we do it...and well too. It's the one skill that is assumed that everyone can do. But it's also the one thing that people constantly complain that others don't do – ask many employees about their bosses, ask many teenagers about their parents, ask many married couples about their spouses.

Instead of listening, most of us are intent on giving advice, giving our opinion or just "sounding off".

Usually what this means, is that when someone is talking to us, instead of really listening, we are usually rehearsing in our head what we are going to say once we can gain a conversational opening. In other words, we maintain a polite silence getting ready to insert our piece into the conversation once the other person stops talking.

Worse still, sometimes we are unable to contain ourselves with the rehearsed speech in our heads and so, we cut-off the other person, interrupt or blurt it out even before they have stopped talking.

Often too, we just hear the first part of the other person's comments and miss the rest. We then get a distorted idea of what they said or just get it plain wrong. Further, we often assume what the other person is saying and jump ahead to form our own conclusions.

Is it any wonder that we misunderstand each other? Is it any wonder that we don't really connect with each other?

However, you probably think of yourself as a reasonably good listener. Most do.

If you asked those at work for their honest opinion, what would they really say? If you asked your family, what would they really say? You might be pleasantly surprised, but all too often, those we work with would say that we need to work on our listening skills. Those we live with no doubt would say the same. Some may even say that we **really** need to work on our listening skills, that we are really poor listeners.

Let me ask you a series of questions:

- What is the one skill that most consultants believe they have, but they actually lack?
- What is the one skill that most managers believe they have, but they actually lack?
- What is the aspect that adolescents say is the number one lack on behalf of parents?
- What is the one skill that due to its absence is almost always at the core of every conflict?
- What is the one skill that, due to its absence, significantly loses sales and income?

- What is the one skill that, due to it's absence, is almost always at the heart of marital or relationship breakdown?
- What is the one skill that is lacking in workplace dis-agreements?
- What is the one skill that separates out effective leaders from non-effective ones?
- What is the one skill that connects people together like no other?
- What is the one skill, that, if we all had it, would mean an entirely different world?

Answer: The ability to listen.

If it's so important, so critical, so vital in business and in life itself, how is it that we don't use this skill or have this ability?

Do you have the courage to fill out **Appendix 1**?

Show some courage and try it out on your staff, your clients, and your family. Remember, "*feedback is the breakfast of champions*". What have you got to lose?

This book is designed to show you how to listen, really listen, and as a result, how to give excellent customer service and further, how to be an effective manager and leader. It might also give you some clues about being the best "you" that you can be.

First Things First

How can you be an effective manager, coach, consultant, adviser, facilitator? How can you be an

effective boss? How can you be an effective leader? How can you be the best that you can be at your job? How can you be penetrating at what you do? How can you make a significant impact on people you counsel, supervise or look after?

Call it what you will – you know the role – it's one where someone comes to you for help or assistance for a product or service or perhaps you are responsible for either someone or a team in terms of their work. It's you and them.

In this book, I may refer to the term "Consultant", but you can substitute the term leader, manager, coach, advisor, professional, facilitator and the sense will be the same.

In fact, you could substitute any job role like lawyer, foreman, teacher, supervisor, accountant, leading hand, site manager, coordinator, chief executive and so on, and the sense would be the same.

In other words, you're in a position where you've got the knowledge, the information and the expertise and somehow, the other person needs or wants or can benefit from that knowledge and expertise. Sometimes too, they don't even know that they need that knowledge or expertise!

So, how do we get to be good at our roles of leading, managing, coaching, and consulting?

First, let's be aware of **four** basics. If you don't understand these, then you won't even get to first base. These are fundamental. Overlook them and you do so at your own peril.

1. First Impressions

How long does it take to make a good **first impression**? What would you guess? I've asked that question numerous times in the MBA Leadership class that I facilitate and I usually get varied responses from 1 second to 2 minutes.

There is little doubt that we make our judgments "snap" judgments.

I've read 7 seconds, I've read 10 seconds. Malcolm Gladwell in his book *"Blink"* indicates that it's about 3 seconds and backs it up with good research evidence. For example, Gladwell compares the intuitive responses of a university class rating a teaching Professor after 3 seconds of observation with responses following the examination of the same Professor after extended time viewing video tapes of the Professor teaching. The result? No difference. The conclusion? That our intuitive first hunches are as good as our prolonged observation and evaluation.

In other words, **you're on before you're on!**

"You don't get a second chance to make a good first impression"

(Author unknown)

So, at a personal level, what does that mean for how you present? What do you need to do to make a good first impression? Do you smile, look at the person in the eyes, have a firm handshake and call them by name?

2. Interpersonal Skills

In the three decades of being a psychologist and dealing with businesses and companies in the commercial and private sector as well as the government sector (both State and Federal), I am convinced that there is at least one packet of skills that most people overlook – interpersonal skills.

I remember reading a small book by John C Maxwell called "*Attitude 101*" about some research conducted by the Stanford Research Institute in the USA where they identified that business success and profit (as well as individual career success and promotion) was attributable to two main factors. Namely, the following:

Technical Skills & Knowledge	**&**	**Interpersonal & Communication Skills**

Now, perhaps you might think that that was not surprising news. Business and career success would no doubt be due to those two factors you might say.

However, the Stanford group went a step further. They were able to attribute a percentage to each factor in relation to how much **each** contributed to success.

What would you guess was the percentage of each factor in regards to its contribution towards success?

The research findings were compelling in this regard.

Technical Skills and Knowledge attributed to only **12.5%** of the success, whereas Interpersonal and Communication Skills attributed **87.5%**.

What does that tell you?

The cynics might say that all you really need is the "gift of the gab" and you'll be okay (and unfortunately in some cases that does happen)! However, the real message is that most of us have concentrated on getting the technical skills, knowledge and information so correct that somehow or other, we have overlooked the importance of the interpersonal and communication skills.

Most of us have been so concerned to get our "piece of paper" such as a Certificate, Diploma or Degree (including the MBA) that we haven't paid much attention to the people skills area.

In a sense, **some of us have just taken that part (ie., interpersonal & communication skills) for granted**.

Certainly, our general secondary and tertiary education sectors haven't helped either in that we have been "brain-washed" into believing that it was all about getting a good grade point average, getting qualifications and gaining knowledge. In part it is.

But in large part, there is another dimension which we haven't been taught and that's how to connect effectively with those around us and how to communicate at an effective level and how to have an impact emotionally.

So, what are those skills in the Interpersonal and Communication area that help us to be effective and to have an impact especially in the work setting?

Everything we do is communication

---

3. Body Language

You need to understand **body language**.

It is said that you can't judge a book by its cover. But we do. What's more, we also judge each other by external appearances. You can argue that that's not respectful of others, that "all that glitters is not glod", that there's more to the person than what you see superficially on the outside and so on. You have probably heard them all. So have I.

The harsh reality though is that it is part of human survival for us to be weighing up our surrounds, and the people in it. Moment by moment we are evaluating what is going on around us, taking in information and sizing up our situation. It is human nature.

Not surprisingly, we naturally weigh up those in our vicinity because we need to know how we might respond and interact with them. We take in data constantly and our radar is constantly scanning our horizon to check how we might react and respond. We measure and note what people say, and how they say it. We evaluate what people do and how they do it. Constantly monitoring and scanning. I read recently that our brain consists of 86 billion neurons and several hundred trillion connections.

Yes, we can't help our brain doing what it's supposed to do.

It is fascinating how many times I have had clients say things like, that "from the moment she comes into the office, we know what kind of day it is going to be" or "he doesn't have to say anything, we just know what kind of a mood he is in". I've heard staff say to me, "the boss isn't in a good mood today so we stay away" or "we have to pick our times when we go to see her" or "we check with his Executive Assistant first to see what kind of mood he's in".

How so? How is it that certain individuals don't have to say anything and yet the staff or others in their environment know exactly what kind of mood that person is in?

This is the power of the non-verbal body language.

4. Verbal & Non-Verbal Communication

You need to understand about verbal versus non-verbal communication.

Let me ask you a question. How much of your communication is verbal and how much is non-verbal? Ever thought about this?

I know that it's not a question that you get asked every day, but nonetheless, it is an important one.

| Verbal Communication (What we say; the Content) | **Vs** | Non-verbal Communication (How we say it; the Emotion) |

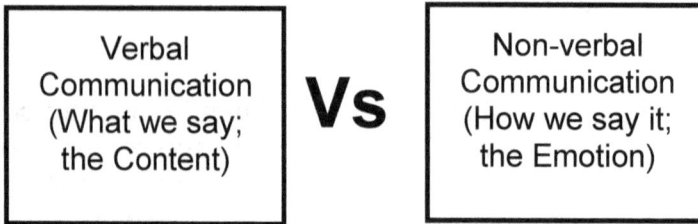

I have asked this question hundreds of times at countless seminars and workshops that I have conducted and I have had every response imaginable from 90% verbal to 10% non-verbal and vice-versa. Most people guess around the 50:50 or 60:40 mark to perhaps 75:25 (in both directions) while a few might guess 80:20 in both directions.

Most though have never really thought about it. Yet it is a critical question. You need to know the answer because communication is at the core of what we do every minute of every day (even when we are **not** talking).

Psychologist Albert Mehrabian has done extensive laboratory measurements on what happens when one person talks to another. Mehrabian conducted some milestone research way back in 1970 where he looked at the question of verbal and non-verbal communication [See L. Longfellow, "Body Talk," *Psychology Today*, October 1970, Vol. 4. No. 5, P.46]. His work has largely stood the test of time although it has been challenged.

What did he find? Verbal communication only accounted for **7%** of the impact whereas Non-verbal accounted for **93%** of the impact.

So, if you remember **10%** verbal and **90%** non-verbal you'll be close to the mark. Even if it's not 10:90 and it's 20:80 or even 25:75, you get the message that there is a lot of communication that is non-verbal.

"Communication is more about what you do than what you say"

(Darryl Cross)

It is true to say that some find it very hard to believe this percentage breakdown. This is because they have generally felt that talking and verbal was always the most powerful. But they would be wrong. It's understandable that they might believe that verbal was the stronger influence because that is what our education system and what our society has led us to believe. However, it is a myth. Good communicators know that already. The rest of us have been very slow to catch up.

Moreover, there is something called the "7 – 38 – 55 Rule". This refers to 7% being the impact of the voice itself, 38% being the impact of the tone of the voice and 55% being the impact of the body language. However, the most important part of the body language is the eyes. The eyes have it. You've heard it said that the "eyes are the windows to the soul". Well, they are the windows to good communication too.

Dan Pink in his book "*A Whole New Mind*" highlights the critical nature of the face and eyes and documents that there are "*43 tiny muscles that tug and stretch and lift our mouth, eyes, cheeks, eyebrows and forehead to convey the full range of human feeling*".

> *"We all, in one way or another, send our little messages out to the world."*
>
> *We say, "Help me, I'm available," "Leave me alone, I'm depressed." And rarely do we send our messages consciously. We act out our state of being with non-verbal body language. We lift one eyebrow for disbelief. We rub our noses for puzzlement. We clasp our arms to isolate ourselves or to protect ourselves. We shrug our shoulders for indifference, wink one eye for intimacy, tap our fingers for impatience, slap our forehead for forgetfulness."*
>
> Julias Fast, *"Body Language"*, 1970

How then are your non-verbals doing?

Ever asked people how you come across non-verbally? Ever asked for feedback about how your face generally looks? How you hold your body? What impression do you really give with your body?

Complete **Appendix 2** if you are courageous enough to gain some important feedback. Who would you ask for feedback? Not just those who you think might like you or say nice things to you. Get a range of feedback. Be brave.

"A conversation is like a painting in that there is a foreground (what is spoken) and a background (the emotions felt) and only when I see both, do I see the whole"

(Author unknown)

Now, follow-up on that initial conversation and ask for more specific feedback.

See **Appendix 3** in order to clarify more directly what it is that people **like** what you do and **not like** what you do.

Remember, **feedback is the breakfast of champions**!

Next question.

How are you going to remember to look approachable, to look friendly, to smile? What prompt do you need to ensure that your exterior is not giving the wrong message? What will remind you to be aware of your externals? In order to change our habits, we all need some physical prompt. Otherwise, we will forget and get caught up again in the busy-ness of life.

One client of mine put a Post-it note on the dashboard of their car so they could see it driving to work. Another bought a new watch-band as a reminder. Another carried some polished stones around in their pocket. Another brought into the office a particular photo that served as a reminder. Use whatever fits for you. But let me say quite clearly, if you don't use a visual prompt in order to remind you, then you won't change your behaviour because you'll forget.

Turn to **Appendix 4** and write down what you will use to prompt you in order for you to be aware of your non-verbals.

Chapter 1 Summary

FIRST THINGS FIRST

Listening. We all think that we do it...and well too. Listening....it's the one skill that is assumed that everyone can do. But it's also the one thing that people constantly complain that others don't do – ask many employees about their bosses, ask many teenagers about their parents, ask many married couples about their spouses.

Instead of listening, most of us are intent on giving advice, giving our opinion, and "sounding off ".

First Things First
Be aware of **four** basics. Overlook these at your peril.

1. First Impressions

How long does it take to make a good **first impression**? Simply put, you're on before you're on!

2. Interpersonal Skills

The Stanford Research Institute reported that there were two packets of skills that were critical to business and career success, namely, "Technical Skills & Knowledge" versus "Interpersonal & Communication Skills".

Not news really, but what is news is the contribution that each plays towards success both in business and career-wise.

Which wins? The Interpersonal & Communication Skills, but read the chapter to find out by how much!

3. Body Language

You need to understand body language.

It is said that you can't judge a book by its cover. But we do. What's more, we also judge each other by external appearances and what we are saying with our body.

4. Verbal & Non-Verbal Communication

How much of your communication is verbal and how much is non-verbal?

It is a critical question. You need to know the answer because communication is at the core of what we do every minute of every day (even when we are **not** talking).

CHAPTER 2:

THE ART OF COMMUNICATION

Yes, we all know how to talk and interact (some admittedly are better connectors than others). However, there is an art to it all.

Sadly though, we have never been taught how to communicate effectively, yet being able to do so is the key to productive and harmonious relationships. Somehow or other, we've just meant to have picked up the ability to communicate well. So, where did we actually learn to communicate? Essentially from our parents or our care-givers or perhaps wider family. Who's to say though, that they were the most effective people in being able to communicate?

The truth is, most of us have had more training in driving a car, baking a cake, or using a computer than we have ever had in learning how to really communicate effectively. It's no wonder we have so many problems in being able to get our message across, in being able to get others to understand our message and getting others to follow our instructions. Further, the education system certainly gave us skills in maths and physics and English, but there was scant attention to communication skills which are really life skills that allow us to be successful.

"The single biggest problem in communication is the illusion that it has taken place"

(George Bernard Shaw)

Communication though is a complex process. It takes time to master it. It's not something that is innate, that we do automatically or in which we have had formal training. But look at the diagram below. If you look at it closely, it's a wonder that any of us get our communication right.

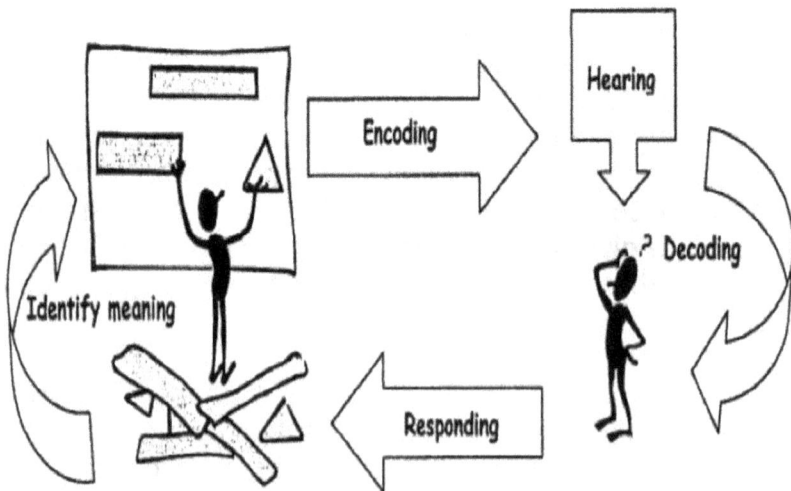

Let's analyse this diagram. In the first instance the sender has to put together the initial communication. This can actually be more difficult than might be anticipated. Just ask anyone who has been angry or hurt or offended and ask them how they put together their initial comments. Irrespective, there are some further traps right in the beginning with the "Encoding" and "Decoding" where our assumptions come into play, our judgements or agendas get in the road, our expectations trip us up, and our filters sift out information.

Then the listener has to respond in such a way that is at best, an approximate representation of what the sender delivered where upon the sender receives that input and has to make meaning of it before the cycle continues round again.

It's a miracle that any of us really understand anyone else!

"Our problem in communicating with friends is that we have an illusion of insight; getting close to someone appears to create the illusion of understanding more than actual understanding"

(Nicholas Epley)

The Basics of Communication

So, what are the principles for being able to communicate well?

As well as what you've understood from above, there are some important messages that you also need to know to assist you on the delicate art of communication.

(1) The way that we start our message often determines the outcome of the conversation

For example, we can expect a very different reaction to starting a conversation with "I" than starting out by saying "You". Note the following examples and see if you can see how it might impact a conversation:

- "I've got a problem in that I'm confused about what has just been said."
- "You didn't explain that very clearly."

Is this just semantics? You might think so, but our natural instinctive reaction is to go into a defensive reaction when someone comes at us with a "you" statement. If we don't go straight to defensive mode, then we'll probably go to fight and push-back mode. Either way, it's not a good omen for a healthy constructive conversation. Occasionally too, some people just shut down altogether and that certainly is not going to assist any conversation.

(2) The way that the message is actually delivered always affects the way that the message is received

Not surprisingly, if the message is delivered with tones that are loud, voice raised, talking quickly with body language just as obvious, then you can quite rightly expect that the words of the message probably won't be received because the way it is delivered is speaking volumes as it were.

So, if you want to be heard, then the onus is on the sender to ensure that they are sending the message in the most positive way possible. We all instinctively know when we are being "got at" or when there is a double message being delivered or when sarcasm is being used, so unless you're deliberately trying to get under someone else's skin, then don't be careless with your message delivery.

(3) The real communication is the message actually received, not the one that you meant to give

Regardless of what you might have intended, the message that the receiver picks up is the real message. Plenty of times, you might have heard yourself (or others) say something like, "But that's not what I meant!" or "I didn't say that!" Well, yes you did, in a manner of speaking (no pun intended).

So it's not what you intended to say or meant to say that counts, it's the way that the other person actually perceives it and takes it on board that counts.

Now, I know that makes it difficult to communicate sometimes because some people have all sorts of blinkers on or they have various personal agendas or they filter everything that someone might say through countless filters, but irrespective, it just means that you need to be aware that it is indeed, the message that is received that is the one that counts.

You need to do everything in your power to ensure that it gets transmitted effectively.

(4) Communication is a two-way street

In other words, it is a shared experience; it's about giving as well as getting. It is certainly not one-way. No-one likes to be talked at. It is hardly a conversation if one person does all the talking.

If you happen to be the talker, then try to ensure that you leave space in the conversation for the other to reply. More importantly, ask them questions about what they think or what they feel and draw them out. Without putting too fine a line on it, it should be a 50:50 experience.

There is a definite sense in which it is a dance. As I say in my workshops, in a way it's a dance like a tango or a waltz. It is certainly not like some of the more modern dance forms where the partners are metres away from each other and each doing their own gyrating thing!

Quite the contrary, this a is a dance of movement in synchronicity; and when you get that right, it is indeed a thing to behold and experience.

Chapter 2 Summary

THE ART OF COMMUNCIAITON

Communication is indeed a complex interplay of factors between the sender of the message and the receiver of the message.

In the middle of all that are our agendas, our filters, judgements, expectations and assumptions which all serve to derail the whole communication process.

The Basics of Communication

There are very important aspects to communication that cannot afford to be overlooked which relate to how the message is begun, how it is delivered, how it is received and overall, it can be likened to a conversational dance.

CHAPTER 3:

LISTENING IN BUSINESS

So, how important is listening in business (both within the public service and commercial enterprise)? How important is it really irrespective of the setting or the environment?

Some **bosses** would suggest that it's really not necessary –
- *"Just tell them what to do."*
- *"They're not paid to think, just do."*
- *"Don't ask them what they want, they'll come up with all sorts of ideas."*
- *"Listening went out with the Ark, now it's about just taking control."*

Some **consultants or advisors** would believe that it's their job to give advice and tell their clients what to do.

- *"After all, that's what they've come to see me for."*
- *"They need me to sort out their problem and fix it up."*
- *"I know what to do, and they need me to do it."*
- *"I haven't got time to listen to them; it's quicker if I just tell them what to do."*
- *"They rely on me for advice."*
- *"If I don't give advice, they'll wonder what they're paying me for."*

In part, this may be true. Employees and clients do rely on good advice. But no-one, no-one, really likes to be told what to do. **It is how they are "told" that makes the difference.**

When managers, consultants and advisors take the trouble to find out staff, customers' or clients' needs or wants and match those needs and wants to a product or service that they have in hand, then the "deal" is done and the transaction occurs.

Once the needs are known, the "deal" then occurs naturally.

Clients are happy to part with their money because their needs are met and they are satisfied. Clients are happy and the consultant is happy.

Two Main Myths

Consultants and advisors suffer from believing **two main myths**.

1. Firstly, much of the consulting philosophy adheres to a notion **that consultants have to "push" a product or service, be the expert and "tell"**, be direct in their marketing and presentation, and somehow "close the sale". It is being maintained here that this is **not** the art of consulting and advising at all. This is at the other end of the continuum of real advising. This is not real consulting. For those who may adhere to this kind of philosophy, they are perpetuating a myth. They are believing a lie.

2. Secondly, there is also the belief that **the success of consulting and advising depends entirely on the brilliance, confidence and persuasive skills of the consultant.** There is also a belief in the market-place that real consulting is all about technique and skills.

It is being maintained here that consulting or advising is **not** dependent on the advisor or consultant. *It is, in fact, dependent on the customer's needs being met irrespective of how "persuasive" the consultant might be and irrespective of any special techniques or selling skills the consultant might have.*

The same goes for managers and leaders in business. If you really want to get your staff engaged, then try listening to them not only to understand their thoughts and feelings, but importantly, understand their ideas and notions about how the business might be run more effectively. You are living in the dark ages as a manager if you truly believe that it's all about telling and directing especially if you are dealing with the younger generation of staff.

The irony though for any manager (public or commercial), is that if you really do take the time and energy to listen to your staff, it is not a waste of resources, and instead, it is maintained here that not only will morale increase, so will productivity and ultimately profit.

In psychology, we are taught that in order to help our client, it is imperative that we show **empathy** or be empathic. This means that we need to, as it were, get inside our client's shoes, stand in their footprints, understand their frame of reference and see the situation from their perspective and their point of view. One of the ways that we do this is to listen and to listen intently.

The response to this notion about "empathy" from many consultants or managers is going to be along the lines of:

- *"That's all right in psychology, but not in business."*
- *"Haven't got time for that kind of stuff in this organisation."*
- *"All sounds a bit Mickey Mouse and too soft for business."*
- *"All you have to do is get them to sign up."*
- *"Don't bother asking clients, just tell them what they need to know."*
- *"Don't bother asking staff, just tell them what they need to know."*

Wrong, wrong, wrong.

If we do not understand our client's frame of reference, and understand where they are coming from, then, we will not be able to provide the help, the cures, the product, the advice, and the tips necessary for them to help themselves move forward in business and in living.

If this holds for clients, then it certainly holds for staff as well.

Of course, too, it follows that if you do not understand your client and appreciate their perspective, then any advice you do give will simply miss the target, will miss the mark, and will leave both you and your client frustrated and discontent. Needless to say, you may well then lose your client.

It is no different in business.

For reasons that are somewhat unclear, in business, we have accepted the assumption that these fundamental principles of interaction and communication, as listed above, suddenly go out the window when we are involved in a commercial transaction. This is hypocrisy! Nothing could be further from the truth.

If you wonder why your consulting is not going well, why your income might be down, and why your strategies and techniques are not working, then, you only need to look at the methods that you are employing in consulting and advising or selling. If you also wonder why consultants often burn out, and become despondent, then again, you need to look closely at their current consulting model and practices.

Training Practices

Traditionally, and for decades, we have employed what could be loosely termed a direct style of advising and consulting. Unfortunately, all of the tertiary training that you might have received either at University or College, at Technical and Further Education or

Vocational Colleges for example, or during in-service training is oriented to giving clients and people advice.

Professionals, including consultants, are trained to do just that, give advice. Be the expert. Tell your clients what they need to know.

What is being maintained here, however, is that **a new style of consulting and selling must be adopted if individuals and companies want to stay profitable in this millennium.** Old style consulting is no longer good enough. How it has survived over numbers of decades is surprising.

Same holds true for being an effective manager. The old days of telling staff what to do was okay for the Industrial era, but in more modern times where people are now trained to think and not just do (like they did in factories), then it is critical that a new style of managing be adopted. The model of the manager being more of a coach is more appropriate to these current times.

Typically, there has been the notion that in order to be a good consultant, one must be the expert, tell, and give direct advice. Clients and people generally though, do not like to be told.

It is probably this sort of approach that means that some consultants, for example, have a general reputation amongst the public that means they are well down the list in terms of regard and respect. This is not to say that old style advising has not worked -- it has, but at what cost?

However, in this new millennium, clients are now more knowledgeable and more informed. The internet has certainly helped in this regard. Clients are now more assertive and know more clearly what they want.

Managers too have felt that it was their role to tell their staff and to give directions. While it is certainly true that at times, it is important to give specific information and to impart certain skills, in the main, it is more important to learn to coach staff in a particular direction. Sadly, in this day and age too, where stresses are increasing and we are being asked to do more with less, some managers have resorted to so much direction and intervention that it has become bullying or harassment.

As an aside, in an age of high technology, there is an increasing trend for people to want what could be loosely termed "high touch".

In other words, while individuals are surrounded by technology which is impersonal, there is a very strong need that there be a very personal side to living as well. So while, on the one hand, we are surrounded by "high tech", there is a very real need within human beings for "high touch". This is another reason why listening, understanding client's or staff's needs and being empathic will be more profitable in the current era and beyond than the old style advising, consulting and managing.

The Consultant Listener

What is the **"Consultant Listener"**? Reference to **Table 1** below highlights in brief, the difference between the two modes of consulting.

Being a consultant or advisor listener means allowing the client to take control of their situation, and allows the consultant to be more of a friend, an ally or coach, rather than someone who is typically seen as an impersonal expert and one being more on the side of the company or their own business.

The consultant listener is someone who can be trusted and who is not a "con" or manipulative simply pushing their own line or the company line. Is it any wonder that many individuals do not come back for return business?

A consultant listener is **not** concerned with statistics and figures and closing a deal. Instead, the consultant is concerned with being more of a friend, establishing a relationship and providing assistance as the client needs it.

Ultimately, there is an intent on providing a personalised service. **It is being maintained here that profits will increase beyond that from which could be expected from the old mode of consulting.**

This is based on **the belief** that being a **Consultant Listener** will mean:

- more opportunities to meet client's needs will be picked up because consultants will listen more intensively to their client's circumstances;

- more return business because clients have had their needs met previously and so, consequently, they will return for more service later;

- that clients will inevitably discuss and talk about their experiences to others which will create new business.

This is based on **the belief** that being an **effective Manager** will mean:

- higher staff morale;

- less absenteeism;

- less staff turnover;

- less conflict and disagreements;

- staff with greater job satisfaction;

- greater outputs and being able to meet key performance indicators;

- staff who are motivated towards their career goals and paths.

Being a consultant listener and an effective manager is the way to go. It is a basic principle of psychology, it is a basic principle of business, it is a basic principle of life.

Failure to move in that direction for companies and consultants will mean a failure to recognise profits. The trends are evident from a number of quarters that service techniques and strategies will need to change dramatically in this era and beyond for companies to do better and survive profitably.

TABLE 1

Old Style Consulting	Vs	Consultant Listener
Instructing	vs	Empathy
Directing	vs	Listening
Statistics	vs	People
Figures	vs	Persons
Salesperson	vs	Friend
Calculating	vs	Caring
Business-Driven	vs	Client-Driven
Self-Driven	vs	Others-Driven
What's in it for me	vs	What's in it for them
This is my story	vs	What's your story?
Structured	vs	Unstructured
Closed	vs	Open
Breadth	vs	Depth
Money	vs	Profit
Company-Centered	vs	Client-Centered
Result	vs	Process
What	vs	How
Pushing	vs	Pulling
Servicing the Firm	vs	Servicing the clients
Fast	vs	Paced

If this is all true, and if profits and repeat business are tied to being a "Consultant Listener", how is it that consultants still adhere to an advising or telling model with their clients? How is it that managers continue to direct and be task-focused rather than coach their staff?

Chapter 3 Summary

LISTENING IN BUSINESS

When managers, consultants and advisors take the trouble to find out staff or clients' needs or wants and match those needs and wants to a product or service that they have in hand, then the "deal" is done and the transaction occurs.

Once the needs are known, the "deal" then occurs naturally. That's the power of "listening" in a business.

Two Main Myths

Consultants and advisors suffer from believing **two main myths**.

1. Firstly, much of the consulting philosophy adheres to a notion **that consultants have to "push" a product or service, be the expert and "tell"**, be direct in their marketing and presentation, and somehow "close the sale". Wrong, wrong, wrong.

2. Secondly, there is also the belief that **the success of consulting and advising depends entirely on the brilliance, confidence and persuasive skills of the consultant.** There is also a belief in the market-place that real consulting is all about technique and skills. Wrong, wrong, wrong.

And two wrongs, don't make a right!

Training Practices

Traditionally, and for decades, we have employed what could be loosely termed a direct style of advising and consulting (and managing). Unfortunately, all of the tertiary training that you might have received either at University or College, or Vocational College or Institute, or through a Training Provider for example, or during in-service training is oriented to giving clients and people advice.

Professionals, including consultants, are trained to do just that, give advice. Be the expert. Tell your clients what they need to know.

What is being maintained here, however, is that **a new style of consulting must be adopted if individuals and companies want to stay profitable in this millennium.** Old style consulting is no longer good enough.

The Consultant Listener

What is the "**Consultant Listener**"?

Being a consultant listener means allowing the client to take control of their situation, and allows the consultant to be more of a friend, an ally or coach, rather than someone who is typically seen as an impersonal expert and one being more on the side of the company or their own business.

The consultant listener is someone who can be trusted and who is not a "con" or manipulative simply pushing their own line or the company line. Is it any wonder that many individuals do not come back for return business?

Same holds true for being an effective manager. The old days of telling staff what to do was okay for the Industrial era, but in more modern times where people are now trained to think and not just do (like they did in factories), then it is critical that a new style of managing be adopted. The model of the manager being more of a coach is more appropriate to these current times.

Reference to **Table 1** highlights in brief, the difference between the two modes of consulting, advising or managing. Which are you?

CHAPTER 4:

WHAT IT IS & WHAT IT IS NOT

Why Don't We Listen?

We all think that somehow we listen. We all somehow think that because we have two ears and we "hear", that we actually listen. The reality is that there are very few people who really listen.

How many people in your life would you really say were prepared to listen to you? Really listen to you. Really understand what you are saying? Really have empathy for your words, your thoughts, your feelings?

How is it that we don't listen? Why not?

1. We Think That We Need to Be "Right"

Many times, these two (ie., being "right" or happy) are mutually exclusive. Let others be right. Why not?

Around 95% of our conflict is not about facts or figures, but about opinion, values or feelings.

Sometimes, you might need to argue about the facts, especially if it is a life and death issue or a health issue or perhaps a major decision regarding business for example. In the main however, most of our arguing is about opinion, values and feelings.

Being right means we have to defend our position – such takes a good deal of time and energy – it means that others get defensive – and it means that we strive to prove them wrong.

Somehow or other we see it as our duty to show others that their position, their point of view, and their opinion is incorrect and that in doing so, somehow or other, they are going to be so appreciative and eternally grateful to you.

Know what? Yes, you guessed it, they are not appreciative at all!

Sometimes there are important issues to do with your life philosophy or your world view on which you may wish to give a perspective, but in the main, it is frequently more appropriate to just let others be right. Can you allow your ego to step back and let others be right? Can you be man or woman enough to permit others to have their point of view?

Change the way you correct people and want to give them the "way it really is" and you'll find that your life will become less defensive and more loving and people will appreciate you more too. Gone will be the days of the battles of the egos – instead you'll be more at peace and so will they.

2. We are Intent on Giving Advice

All of our training, secondary and tertiary, professional and trade training is directed to giving advice.

Think about it. Accountants, bankers and financial planners are taught to give advice. So are nurses, doctors, lawyers, architects, marketers, advertising agents, physiotherapists and so on. So are plumbers, electricians, carpenters, builders, interior decorators, chefs, designers and on it goes. We are all taught to give direction and give advice.

We tend to do this as a matter of course. It is almost as though it is at the core of our substance. It is almost as though it is second nature to give advice. We all seem to know about "stuff" and somehow need to tell others about it. It may have been "stuff" that we learnt through our training or it may have been knowledge that we picked up informally through our hobbies, through informal courses, through conversation with others or through our experiences. Regardless, we feel that our knowledge and information needs to be passed on.

For example, go into the local butcher shop, have a casual talk to your neighbour or have an informal chat to your auntie and let slip that you're perhaps not feeling well and that you're a "bit off colour" and what do you immediately receive? Advice. It could be as many and as varied as eating and sleeping properly, to going home to take a Panadol and lie down, to visiting your naturopath for extra vitamins, to going to your general practitioner for a flu shot and on it goes. Everyone's got advice.

Somehow or other too, we all seem to think that we have a monopoly on the truth. We know how it should be for the other person. We know what should work for them. We have the exact advice that will fix their problem. We leap in with what we think is good advice. We might be well-intentioned, but unfortunately, what works for us doesn't always work for others. One mould does not fit for all. The cap does not fit for all.

Instead, we would do more of a service to listen. We would be of more benefit to the other person if we listened and understood their perspective and clarified their thoughts and feelings. We would also endear ourselves to others more if we listened.

3. We like to Hear the Sound of Our Own Voice

Ego gets in the road. We like to be the centre of our world. We artificially inflate ourselves with our own importance when we push our advice. We know it all. We feel good because we have the whole thing "sown up". We "puff" ourselves up.

We tend to rail-road others with our advice and perhaps bombard them with our knowledge and superior information and expertise.

Often these kind of people can also talk in a condescending way and make you feel that they have the "right and proper" answer. They may give the impression that they are superior and above you in some way.

If, for some reason, you might consider disagreeing with them, they will generally try to make you look stupid simply because they are "right" and you are "wrong". Their ego is involved.

4. We Have Never been Taught How to Listen

Does that sound strange? Think about it. You certainly were told to "listen" when your parents or teachers were talking to you or giving you instructions. You were certainly given reprimands such as "What's the matter with you, can't you listen?" But did anyone actually ever tell you what it really meant to listen?

How many classes did you ever attend on listening? How many lessons did you ever have in how to listen?

Sometimes your mother, father, guardian or teacher might have said to you, "Now, what did I just say to you?" or "Repeat what I just said." Other than that, the lessons on listening were sparse.

It was just assumed that somehow or other, we could all do it. It was assumed that because we could hear with our ears, that we could automatically listen.

Nothing is further from the truth.

---

*"The good Lord gave you two ears
and one mouth and you should use
them in that proportion."*

(Author unknown)

Having ears and hearing is not listening. Listening is not the same as hearing. "Hearing" is really a passive act which really does not require you to participate. In contrast, "listening" is an active act which demands your real attention and your energy.

You know as well as I do, that if you stop and think about it, you can hear every word of the statement and yet have not paid a skerrick of attention to it. You heard with your ears, but you did not listen.

5. We believe that Listening is for "Softies" or is too Esoteric

There is still a belief in some companies that essentially comes out of the Industrial Age when we controlled people and used them for their physical labour (and didn't have to worry about their heads or their hearts), and so, we still need to be direct and authoritative with people. "Tell them what they need to know."

Perhaps underlying these consultants and managers is a hint of the dictator or the bully. Maybe they also pride themselves on being from the "old school" where its always been done this way ie., being dictatorial.

Generally speaking, and unfortunately so, these people seem entrenched in their ways and tend to cause much stress amongst their staff or their customers. What would it take for them to understand that they ostracise people, that they turn people away, that they lose sales and they lose staff?

6. We have our own Prejudices, Agendas & Beliefs

When someone else might be speaking, we are consumed by our own filters, assumptions or biases which affects what we hear. We all listen through filters of various kinds and unfortunately, we are generally unaware of them most of the time.

When someone might say a particular word or phrase or give a particular view-point, our prejudices and our beliefs kick in and we end up listening to our own inner voices and tuning out the other person or defending in our heads our position.

Listening Bad Habits

What are the main bad habits that prevent good listening?

How do you fare on the following?

- **Jumping in and reassuring**
  Trying to smooth things over or pacify might be well-intentioned, but it's not helping at all with listening.
  "There there, it will be alright"
  "I'm sure it's nothing to worry about"
  "It will be OK"

- **Giving advice**
  Everyone has good advice on just about everything and somehow or other, everyone seems to be an expert on everything.

"If I was you, what I'd do is..."
"What you should do is..."
"You ought to try..." etc

- **Interrupting**
  Research shows that the average individual listens for only 17 seconds before interrupting – and we wonder why we can't listen?

- **Intellectualising / Spiritualising**
  Having an academic answer or sharing a philosophy or theoretical perspective or quoting formal sources is not at all helpful – who cares really when it's actually about listening to a person's emotions or listening to the story that they want to give you?

- **Going off on a tangent**
  "You think you've got problems, well, when I was...."
  "That's nice, but when I...."
  "That reminds me of the time..."

- **Rehearsing in our head what we will say when we get a conversational opening**
  This is the big one. Most of the time most of us are so intent on rehearsing in our head what we are going to say as soon as we can grab a conversational opening that we have little time for really listening. We are focused on framing our words in our mind so we can give our point of view, or give our advice, or give our words of wisdom that we actually block out what the other person is saying.

These are the most common bad habits that stop us from really listening and they get in the way of the speaker being able to say what is really on their mind. How many might you be guilty of? Perhaps instead, you've noticed others around you fall into these traps.

In short, they are a No-No!

What is Listening?

Have you ever had the experience of having someone tell you that they are a really good listener or that they are good with people, but within a very short while in conversation, you realise that quite the opposite is true?

"Seek first to understand, then to be understood"

(Dr Stephen Covey)

I remember once running a therapy group a long time back and one woman in the group introduced herself and indicated that she felt one of her strengths was being a "a good listener", but in the very next group exercise, she could not remember her partner's name that she had just been talking to previously nor anything about her! So exactly what is listening?

What It Is Not

"Listening" is **not** any one of the following:

1. **Maintaining a polite silence:** listening does not mean simply maintaining a polite silence while you are rehearsing in your head the speech you are going to make the next time your partner stops talking and you grab a conversational opening.

2. **Mowing others down:** listening does not mean waiting alertly for flaws in the other person's arguments so that later you can mow him or her down.

3. **Having all the answers and giving advice:** listening does not mean that you are supposed to come up with all the necessary answers to problems or issues or be especially knowledgeable and wise and sophisticated. Regardless, can you ever know "what is best" for the other person when they have a totally different life experience from you?

4. **Giving inappropriate minimal responses:** listening is not simply a case of saying "I see" or "yes" or "uh-huh" at various pauses or at specific times in the conversation when you think it seems appropriate to do so.

5. **Playing "psychiatrist":** listening is not trying to be insightful and interpretive and kind of "big dealing" yourself by being in touch with the latest theories on human dynamics and human development.

6. **Parroting:** listening is not regurgitating back to your partner word for word what you have directly heard

like a recorder play-back does nor does it mean being like a "parrot".

7. **Sympathy:** listening is not showing sympathy **for** a person nor feeling **for** the other person.

8. **Automatic skill:** listening is not just something that comes naturally, where everyone is just sort of born with it and everyone has an in-built ability to be able to listen and communicate with others around them.

What It Is

1. **Empathy:** listening is being able to show empathy for a person, which means experiencing with the other what they feel and think. This means entering actively and imaginatively into the other person's situation and trying to understand a frame of reference and a perspective different from your own.

   It means not only hearing the words, but picking up the feeling tones, even perhaps the meaning that might be somewhat hidden for the speaker. Can we sense the shape of the other person's inner world? Can we put ourselves in their shoes and appreciate what it is like to be them?

   In the novel, "To Kill a Mockingbird", listening appropriately to another person is described as the ability to jump inside the skin of the other person and walk around and see the world through the eyes of the other.

2. **Asking questions:** a good listener does not merely remain silent, but is prepared to ask questions without

any hint of scepticism or challenge or hostility (whether in wording or non-verbally).

Such questions need to be clearly motivated by genuine curiosity about the speaker's view and as such could be called "questions for clarification". These questions simply request more information (eg., "Can you expand on that point?" "Can you state that argument again?")

3. **Giving feedback:** the listener must communicate to the other that he or she has heard and critically, this needs to be done in a non-judgemental, accepting, non-evaluative and caring way. Therefore, saying things like, "What you are really saying is..." or "Summarising what you've said..." allows the other person to know if you are "on target" and are correct in what you consider you have heard.

4. **A learned skill:** it is not innate, but is an acquired skill that has to be practised and worked at (like many other skills in life).

Redemptive and Creative

Being able to intensively listen to another is a gift. It is truly redemptive to others and creative.

Redemptive because when someone really hears us and sensitively understands, it frees us from the fear of ourselves and our inadequacies and feelings of lack of self-worth. It shows respect for the other person. It gives a message that they count, their opinions count and their feelings count.

Redemptive because we become more whole and re-own those parts of us that we have previously shut away. Creative because it unleashes new energy in us to grow, to find new goals to reach, to find new solutions to issues. It encourages us to move on and continue to be our best and manage the challenges in life.

Listening is a very real gift. It's one that is given to all of us if we wish to use it and practise it and its power is absolutely profound. **Are you using your gift?**

This might seem all a bit too "soft" for business using our "gifts" such as listening.

As I said, our greatest handicap in life is ourselves in that we cut off through our filters things that could well be of significant benefit to us.

Leave your mind open and put your filters down and your agendas away.

What have you got to lose? If you really give listening a go, a real go, and apply this new consulting model and it doesn't work, you can go back to your old way of doing things.

As I said, what have you got to lose?

> # Chapter 4 Summary

WHAT IT IS & WHAT IT IS NOT

Why Don't We Listen?

How is it that we don't listen? Why not?
1. **We Think That We Need to Be "Right"**
2. **We are Intent on Giving Advice**
3. **We like to Hear the Sound of Our Own Voice**
4. **We Have Never been Taught How to Listen**
5. **We believe that Listening is for "Softies" or is too Esoteric**
6. **We have our own Prejudices, Agendas & Beliefs**

Listening Bad Habits

What are the main bad habits that prevent good listening? There are five main ones that stop us from listening and that get in the way of us effectively communicating.

What is Listening?

What It Is Not
There are eight separate things that are not considered to be listening.

What It Is

There are four separate aspects that are considered to constitute listening.

Redemptive and Creative

Being able to intensively listen to another is a gift. This might seem all a bit too "soft" for business using our "gifts" such as listening. But what have you got to lose?

If you really give listening a go, a real go, and apply this new consulting model and it doesn't work, you can go back to your old way of doing things.

CHAPTER 5:

WHAT ARE THE SKILLS?

The Levels of Listening

There are various levels of listening. It is important to recognise that there is just not one level. There are actually five levels. Let's name them.

1. Ignoring. This really doesn't need any explanation. It's fairly self-evident.

2. Pretending. This is recognised by responses like "yeah", "uh-huh," "right."

3. Selective Listening. This is recognised by the person who only hears certain parts of the conversation. Most of us are guilty at times of doing this.

4. Active Listening. This is when the person pays attention to the words being said.

5. Empathic Listening. This is listening with intent to really understand what is being said and to really understand the feelings being expressed.

The Skills of Listening

Basically, there are **eight specific skills** that make up listening.
1. Pay Attention & Don't Interrupt
2. Suspend Your Judgment
3. Paraphrase
4. Acknowledge their Feelings
5. Summarise
6. Ask Questions
7. Find out What is Most Important
8. Help Them Work Out What has to Happen

It's true to say though that skills 1 to 5 are the most important. If you don't get those right, you can forget the other three. Let's take each in turn.

1. Pay Attention & Don't Interrupt

Paying attention is putting aside what you are doing, turning to face the person, and making eye contact.

"The way that we start our conversation often determines the outcome of the communication"

The eye contact does not need to be "staring", but comfortable. Maintain eye contact and do not do something else at the same time (eg., flick over some pages, glance at the monitor or screen, watch the TV etc).

Facial expression needs to be relaxed and perhaps smiling. At least you don't want to look poker-faced. It is important to non-verbally indicate that you are giving the person your time and attention. Remember, your non-verbals say a whole lot!

2. Suspend Your Judgment

Suspension of judgement is when you put your own views or your own agendas to one side. In other words, the consultant or manager attempts to understand the other person's situation without imposing his or her own assumptions and values on it all. Don't be too quick to judge. Don't be too quick to evaluate.

This takes patience and respect.

The consultant or manager must demonstrate an attitude of what is called 'unconditional positive regard' toward the other person whether that be a client, customer or staff member. The listener makes his or her attention available independent of the other person's behaviour. This serves to assure the other person that the listener will listen without imposing conditions on their opinions or behaviour.

In actual terms, suspending judgement involves allowing time for **the other person's message to sink in** without trying to make decisions about it or jumping to conclusions about their issue or jumping in at all.

The listener who suspends judgement is likely to...

- check out his or her assumptions (*"Are you really saying that....?"*)
- request clarification from the other person (*"I'm not sure what you meant by.....?"*)
- endeavour to understand the meanings the other person places on the particular issue issue or situation.

Suspending judgement communicates respect and acceptance to the other person.

Of course we all have judgements and opinions about other people and what they might have said or done. However, in this "listening conversation", such opinions are put at the back of the mind and not at the front of the mind. In other words, while we hold our opinions, we do not let them out, we do not say them and we "reserve judgment".

3. Paraphrasing

In **paraphrasing**, the consultant or manager attempts to feed back to the client or staff member the essence of what he or she has just said, but in a restated form.

Paraphrasing often centres more on **what** the other person said than **how** they said it. Paraphrasing is useful in clarifying confusing verbal content, in tying together a number of recent comments and in highlighting issues by stating them more concisely.

Paraphrasing content achieves **four** specific purposes:

(1) It **conveys** to the other person that the listener is with the person and is trying to understand what the person is saying.

(2) It helps to **crystallize** a person's comments by repeating what he or she has said in a more concise manner, and in the listener's own words.

(3) It provides **a check** for the listener's own perceptions and verifies whether or not the listener really does understand what the other person is saying.

(4) It helps the other person **to move further** and talk more extensively on the topic.

This skill is really a first basic step.

It is relatively easy to do. It is simply giving feedback to the other person about what you think that you just heard. Having said that, although it might be the easiest step, most just don't do it. Strange.

Now turn to **Appendix 5** and practice writing down some paraphrases to the cue statements provided.

Of course this might be seen as somewhat superficial writing it down on paper, but experience is a wise teacher and I can tell you that if you cannot do it on paper, there is absolutely no way that you will ever do it in real life.

Besides, the discipline of writing it down means that your brain "gets it" easily and the neural pathways to learning this "new" skill start to take shape.

4. Acknowledge their Feelings

This skill involves being alert to and responding to the **feeling** being expressed, rather than attending solely to the **content** of what the person says.

It is the ability to be with the person emotionally. It is therefore a very powerful skill. Not only is it important to paraphrase what you heard as we discussed above, but to also reflect back the feelings in full.

What the other person is saying is the *content* portion of the message being communicated, but one must also listen to **how** the person says what he or she does. For example:

- the person may speak more quickly when communicating enthusiasm,
- wave their hands around when being excited,
- look down with shoulders hunched over when communicating being "down",
- move slowly when communicating discouragement and so forth.

Alternatively, the person may use specific feeling words such as 'depressed', 'down', 'anxious', 'tense', 'annoyed', 'stressed-out' or 'happy'.

Being alert to and responding to the feeling being expressed is a skill which is appropriate at most times:

- regardless of the nature of the feeling (whether it is positive, negative or 'in-between'), and

- regardless of the direction of expression (towards ones-self, towards others, the listener or the 'consulting' situation).

Of all the skills, *this one of **Acknowledging their Feelings** is the hardest.* Why?

It is the most difficult because it creates most "fear" amongst people simply because consultants and managers believe that they cannot control emotions and feelings and they believe that it might all "get out of control" (and that would be awful!). This is a myth because clients and staff won't allow themselves to get out of control anyway.

Furthermore, **the real reality is that if the consultant and manager do tap into the emotion, the other person will feel listened to like no other skill can do**. The real question then, is whether the consultant or the manager has the courage to use the reflection of feeling. Are they up for it?

As an aside, being a psychologist meant that during my days of clinical consulting, I would often engage in marital counselling and without doubt, it was this skill of Acknowledging Feelings alone that could turn marriages around. Typically the males were terrible at it, and the females yearned for it. When the males were brave enough to venture into this emotional arena, their women were delighted (and it's certainly true to say, that there were a good proportion of males who also longed for someone to listen to their emotions too).

Now try **Appendix 7** and see how you go formulating some reflective feeling responses.

5. Summarise

Summarising is when the consultant or manager attends to a broader range of events and information than in a straight paraphrase or acknowledging of feelings. It's simply pulling it all together.

In summarizing the other person's experience, the listener attempts to:

- Restate / repeat / reproduce
- Condense, and
- Clarify the other person's experience.

A summary covers a relatively longer time period (than, a paraphrase), eg., it puts together a number of statements, an entire phase of a session, or even an entire interview.

Summarizing serves **three** important functions:

(1) It helps **to crystallize** what the other person has been talking about. When the listener draws together both the feeling and content expressed throughout the session, the listener helps the other person to focus on the issues which most concern him or her.

(2) It serves **to stimulate** further talk on the issue, and at a potentially deeper level.

(3) It provides an opportunity for the listener to verify whether or not he or she is **perceiving** the other person correctly.

6. Ask Questions

Asking key questions and following up on what the other person has just said is a powerful way to gain empathy and understanding as well as show that you're really listening. We will say more about this area in a separate chapter, but it is important to cover it briefly here.

After all, you can't ask a question effectively if you're not listening.

- Often it can be helpful to ask clarifying questions eg., "Could you tell me more about that?" "What did you mean exactly when you said ...."
- Once you consider that you have heard ALL that needs to be said, ask, "What do you think is the most important aspect to what you've been saying?"
- "What do you think you'd like to do about what you've just said?" or "Is there anything you'd like to do about what you just said?"
- "Is there anything more that you'd like to add?"

7. Find out What is Most Important

After you have listened to the client or staff member, ask **"What is the most important part of what you have been saying?"** or "What do you consider is the key to what you just said?"

This serves to crystallise what they have said and to ensure that you have heard it clearly. Remember to wait for their re?sponse and again, feedback what you just heard (either by a paraphrase or acknowledging their feelings, or both).

8. Help Them Work Out What has to Happen

The final question in this listening conversation is this, **"Now that you're said what the issue is, what would you like me, or you, or both of us, to do about it?"**

You may need to give the client, customer, the staff member or employee some space to think about this. Be patient. Once they have finished, again, feedback what you just heard to make sure that you're both agreed on the direction forward.

Of course, that doesn't mean that you can't also impart what you consider could be a solution or a fix, but it's allowing the other person the opportunity to say first what might work for them or to gauge what their opinion on the matter might be. This ensures too that they have buy-in and that they are not just dumping an issue on you as their consultant or manager, but that they too have a part in resolving it.

Chapter 5 Summary

WHAT ARE THE SKILLS?

The Levels of Listening

There are various levels of listening. It is important to recognise that there is just not one level. There are actually five levels.

The Skills of Listening

Basically, there are **eight specific skills** that make up listening. The first five skills are absolutely key. Without them, you can forget the last three skills.

1. Pay Attention & Don't Interrupt
2. Suspend Your Judgment
3. Paraphrase
4. Acknowledge their Feelings
5. Summarise
6. Ask Questions
7. Find out What is Most Important
8. Help Them Work Out What has to Happen

CHAPTER 6:

ASKING POWERFUL QUESTIONS

The Power is in the Question

What is it about questions that make them so important in any conversation let alone the conversations that consultants and leaders must engage in on a daily basis? You see, questions by their very nature, engage the other person. It's not like 'telling' or 'giving advice' where the other person can disregard what you have to say or simply tune you out.

Instead, a question entices people into the conversation. Asking a question means that the brain can't help itself. The brain is programmed and designed to find answers, fix 'stuff' and find solutions. That's its business. That's what it's good at. So, naturally enough when a question is asked, the brain immediately engages to try to find the answer.

Asking a question engages people. *But asking a powerful question engages powerfully.* So what is a powerful question? One that makes people think. You certainly know that you've asked a powerful question when the other person says, "That's a good question." What they mean is that your question is making them stop and think. They are therefore thinking in a domain or area that they haven't considered before or they are having to reach into arenas where they need to consider options or viewpoints or actions that they haven't encountered before.

Asking a question and gaining a response means that you as a consultant and manager are also getting buy-in from the other.

At times, I have heard the suggestion too that asking questions is somehow a sign of weakness in that the individual is supposed to know all the answers. Somehow, asking a question is a reflection of incompetency. However, effective leadership means that you need information and knowledge and the other person may have such information that is imperative to effective decision-making and critical to you doing your role.

"Leadership is not so much about knowing the right answers, as it is about knowing the right questions"

(Author unknown)

In my experience, what separates leaders from the really successful ones is the ability not only to listen effectively, but to ask questions, yes, powerful questions.

Problem Questions

Before we consider what might be really good questions, let's see what makes up a poor question. These questions stifle conversation and tend to lead the conversation in a specific direction.

Closed Questions

Open questions allow the respondent to contribute meaningfully to the conversation and elicits their opinion and their input. This kind of question encourages the other person to develop their answer in whatever length and in whatever detail that they wish.

For example:
- "How is the project going?"
- "What do you think needs to happen next?"
- "How do you feel about that?"
- "Can you give me a specific example?"
- "Can you tell me more about that?"
- "What kind of experience have you had in sales?"

This means that the other person is invited to give their perspective and this opens up the dialogue.

Contrast this with a **closed question** which really only elicits essentially a "Yes" or "No" response or at best, a very limited response. For example:

- "Is the project coming in on time?"
- "Do you want Bob on the project?"

- "If you were in charge of the meeting, wouldn't you handle it differently?"
- "Do you get along with him?"
- "Do you like the group that you're working with now?"
- "How long have you worked in sales?"

Of course, sometimes closed questions are very necessary especially in times of crisis or when things need to happen quickly, but generally, they do not facilitate the conversation.

Forced Choice Questions

The forced choice question might also be described as the 'either-or' question because it limits the other person's choices. They might prefer none of the choice offered, but somehow have to make a choice from the selection offered. This is really about the questioner dictating terms or directing the conversation in their intended direction.

For example:
- "Are you going to procrastinate over this report or are you going to start to work on it?"
- "Do you want to come in early today or stay later tonight?"

Double-barrelled questions

These are questions where one question is asked on top of the other. It's confusing. Does the other person answer the first question or the second one? If they manage to answer both, have they done the answer justice when the person has crammed two answers together in the one comment.

- "You said that you strongly disagreed with some of the instructions; would you like to give me an example and tell me why"?
- "How do you think that we can get this project back on track and do you think that we need to bring Brian into it?"

Leading Questions

In this kind of question, the questioner is not really asking a question, or really seeking information, but instead is offering an opinion.

For example questions like:
- "Don't you think that...?"
- "Wouldn't you agree that...?"
- "Isn't it true that...?"
- "Don't you want to ...?"
- "You wouldn't want that would you?"
- "You'd have to agree that...?"

They all have a direct implicit message.

The questioner attempts to build the answer into the question to get what she or she wants. Generally there is no alternative to the answers suggested by the question itself.

Demanding Questions

Some questions are asked in such a way that they actually make a demand. Take for example:

- "Have you done anything about...?"
- "When are you going to...?"

These questions do not ask for information, but rather have an implicit demand.

"Got'cha" Questions

Now we come to the "got'cha" question which was originally derived from Eric Berne's book "*Games People Play*" published way back in 1964 which has the theme of "Now I got'cha, you clown". This question is largely a set-up such as:

- "Weren't you the one who...?"
- "Didn't you say that...?"
- "Didn't I see you...?"

The person asking the question is all about trapping the other person. They do not really want an answer to their question at all. Instead, they want to dig a hole for the other person to fall into and then maybe try to bury them!

The more exaggerated form of this question is the one where the respondent is judged no matter which way they tend to answer the question. For example:

- "Have you stopped drinking excessively?"

- "Are you still dating all the females on this floor?"
- "Have you managed to get a report in on time yet?"

The 'Why' Question

The "why" question is always a problem.

The truth is that most people don't why they do the things that they do. Does the person who is frequently late to work know exactly what's bringing this about? Does the person who is aggressive towards their work peers know exactly what this aggression is all about?

In my experience, asking a "why" question only elicits a "story" or an excuse. How come? Well, we all have a brain and we all expect that we need to know the answers to the kind of questions asked of us, and that includes the "why" question. Frequently when it is used, an individual can become defensive and feel the need to come up with some sort of justification or explanation. The "why" question is typically followed by a "because" statement where the person is forced to rationalise and defend themselves. Hence, the "story".

Early in my career, I did a good deal of clinical work with children and conducted parenting programs and then later ran a hospital unit for children with behaviour disorders (which both prompted writing the book on *"Growing Up Children"*). It always used to amuse me that when the little brother, say, hit his little sister or misbehaved in some way, that the parents would immediately ask, "Why did you hit her?" What are the parents expecting exactly? Are they expecting the child to stop, pause, show considered reflection and then reply with something like, "That's a very good question mum (or dad) and I'd have to say that my instinctual ego impulses which have been there since birth suddenly took over...etc"

Little children don't know the answers to these "why" questions and big children called adults don't always know either.

While there is no doubt a reason behind every behaviour, it is highly unlikely that the "why" question will help an individual discover this reason.

Instead, the better question is the one that starts with "What", How", and "When". But more about this later.

"Questions are the golden keys that unlock hearts and minds"

(Author unknown)

Effective Questions

If "why" questions are ineffective, then what is a better question? As mooted above, the what, how or when questions are far better. This is because by their very nature, they bring about a more specific response. As I've said in many a workshop, ask a dumb question and you'll get a dumb answer!

For instance, notice the difference between "Why are you late?" versus "What caused you to be late? or "What made you late?" Is this just semantics? The question is more likely to elicit behaviours and feelings rather than rationalisations coming from any sort of defensiveness.

If you had to ask only one question of your boss, staff, clients or customers, then it would be:

- "What do you think?"

Once the other person has given a response, be prepared to listen intently and then ask further follow up questions like "Anything else?"

The key really is to listen (using the skills in Chapter 5) and then ask simple follow-up questions. Classic questions in this regard are:

- "What do you mean by that?"
- "Tell me more."

However, perhaps you could contemplate the following list and maybe adopt a few to begin with as you start to create new communication habits.

Beginning the Conversation

1. Starting the Actual Session
- What's occurred since we last spoke?
- What would you like to talk about?
- What's new / the latest / the update?
- How was your week?
- How's life? How's work?

2. Clarification
- What do you mean?
- What does it feel like?
- What seems to confuse you?
- Can you say more?
- What do you want?

3. Example
- Will you give an example?
- For instance?
- Like what?
- Such as?
- What would it look like?

4. Elaboration
- Will you elaborate?
- Will you tell me more about it?
- What else?
- Is there more?
- What other ideas do you have about it?

5. For Instance
- If you could do it over again, what would you do differently?
- If I were you, what would you have done?
- How else could a person handle this?
- If you could do anything you wanted, what would you do?
- For instance?

6. Exploration
- May we explore that some more?
- Would you like to brainstorm this idea?
- What other angles can you think of?
- What is just one more possibility?
- What are your other options?

7. Substance

- What seems to be the trouble?
- What seems to be the main obstacle?
- What is stopping you?
- What concerns you the most about .....?
- What do you want?

Looking at Options

1. Options

- What are the possibilities?
- If you had your choice, what would you do?
- What are possible solutions?
- What if you do and what if you don't?
- What options can you create?

2. Outcomes

- What do you want?
- What is your desired outcome?
- If you got it, what would you have?
- How will you know you have reached it?
- What would it look like?

3. Predictions

- How do you suppose it will all work out?
- What will that get you?
- Where will this lead?
- What are the chances of success?
- What is your prediction?

4. Resources

- What resources do you need to help you decide?
- What do you know about it now?

- How do you suppose you can find out more about it?
- What kind of picture do you have right now?
- What resources are available to you?

Seeking to Bring About Some Action

1. Implementation
- What is the action plan?
- What will you have to do to get the job done?
- What support do you need to accomplish...?
- What will you do?
- When will you do it?

2. Planning
- What do you plan to do about it?
- What is your game plan?
- What kind of plan do you need to create?
- How do you suppose you could improve the situation?
- Now what?

3. Taking Action
- What action will you take? And after that?
- What will you do? When?
- Is this a time for action? What action?
- Where do you go from here? When will you do that?
- What are your next steps? By when?

Concluding the Conversation

1. Integration
- What will you take away from this?
- How do you explain this to yourself?
- What was the lesson?
- How can you lock in the learning?
- How would you pull all this together?

2. Summary
- What is your conclusion?
- How is this working?
- How would you describe this?
- What do you think this all amounts to?
- How would you summarize the effort so far?

There is little doubt that being an effective listener also means being able to ask powerful questions that make people think and don't cause them to be defensive or just give an excuse or a "story".

Listening skills and question technique go together just like the forefinger and thumb work together to produce a result.

Really, they are inseparable. If you're intent on being not just a leader, but an influential leader, then learn how to ask thoughtful questions.

Chapter 6 Summary

ASKING POWERFUL QUESTIONS

The Power is in the Question

Asking a question engages people. But asking a powerful question engages powerfully. So what is a powerful question? One that makes people think.

Problem Questions

Closed Questions
Forced Choice Questions
Double-barrelled Questions
Leading Questions
Demanding Questions
Got'cha Questions
The 'Why' Question

Effective Questions

If "why" questions are ineffective, then what is a better question? As discussed in the chapter, the what, how or when questions are far better. This is because by their very nature, they bring about a more specific response.

Beginning the Conversation
Looking at Options
Seeking to Bring About Some Action
Concluding the Conversation

Listening skills and question technique go together just like the forefinger and thumb work together to produce a result. Really, they are inseparable. If you're intent on being not just a leader, but an influential leader, then learn how to ask thoughtful questions.

CHAPTER 7:

THE KNOWING DOING GAP

Increase All The Bottom Lines

You may well understand now that being able to effectively listen is a key to career and business success as well as have the ability to ask powerful or thoughtful questions. There is a direct pay-off to improved customer and client relationships which leads to increased profits and inevitably, to job satisfaction. There is also a very significant pay-off to your staff who will feel that you care and are supporting them.

Now, you might know that and you might understand that, but what will make you actually do it? What would allow you make it start to happen?

What would allow you to do it sufficiently often to make it become a habit? – a good habit – a good communication habit.

You might know what to do, but there may well be a "gap" to you actually doing it. How will you actually bridge the gap between you knowing that you ought to listen and you wanting to listen more, to you actually doing it and then becoming good at it?

"Life rewards actions, not good intentions"

(Darryl Cross)

Most of us, most of the time are well-intentioned. We think about it, we intend to do something about it, but it never quite eventuates.

What separates those who are successful in life and those who are not? Those who actually take steps and make it happen, step by step.

Remember that in life and in business there are no short-cuts – it is DISCIPLINE that is required if you really want to change your communication habits, be an effective listener leading you to being an effective consultant, manager or leader.

"Discipline is the bridge between goals and accomplishments"

(Jim Rohn)

What is the definition of "stupidity"? **Answer:** Doing the same thing you did yesterday and expecting different results. Don't fall into that trap. Do it differently.

---

*"If you do what you've always done,
you'll get what you always got"*

(Author unknown)

You have a responsibility to yourself and those around you (your clients, your customers, your staff) to be the best that you can be which allows them in turn, to be the best that they can be.

---

*"If you want to be something different,
you have to do something different "*

(Author unknown)

Overcoming the Barriers

So, what would get in the road of you practising your listening and questioning skills? Remember, that no-one gets good at something unless they make a determined effort to practice. No matter what it is.

What **barrier** would stop you from practising your listening skills?

- **Simply forget?**
  Then give yourself a visual reminder such as a post-it note, or a reminder on your PC, or perhaps buy a new watch band as a way to remind yourself, or even a new pen which will serve as a prompt to remember to

listen. In other words, your visual prompt doesn't have to be obvious to everyone – just to you.

- **Not enough time** – too many other things to think about and do?

  Then you are not making this a priority and are really saying that other things are more important. Are they really? Sure you might be pressed for deadlines and there may be demands on you, but how's that different from any other time? Those demands and deadlines are not going to suddenly stop or go away.

  What would it take for you to organise a time in your diary to practise?

  Furthermore, you could actually practise your listening skills as you went about your day anyhow. Then, it wouldn't incur any "extra" time. It could become part of your day and part of your interactions. Imagine how your Emotional Intelligence rating would increase as people saw you as more attentive and really listening.

- **No-one to practice with**
  Isn't it great that you have a whole world out there waiting for someone to really listen to them. From bus drivers, shop owners, to the guy in the lift and the colleague in the next office. Sure, they might very well be brief conversations, but all you need is a sentence or a comment from someone (anyone!) and you can practice a listening response.

  Okay now, no more excuses, no more barriers. As the Nike saying goes, "Just do it!" and watch your world get turned upside down.

And don't be surprised if someone says something like, "Gee you've changed" or words to that effect.

Go on try it. What have you got to lose?

> **Chapter 7 Summary**

THE KNOWING DOING GAP

Increase All The Bottom Lines

You may well understand now that being able to effectively listen is a key to career and business success. There is a direct pay-off to increased customers and clients which leads to increased profits and inevitably, to job satisfaction.

Overcoming the Barriers

So, what would get in the road of you practising your listening skills? Remember, that no-one gets good at something unless they make a determined effort to practice. No matter what it is. So, go and get good at it!

APPENDICES

APPENDIX 1

LISTENING SURVEY

Try to honestly answer the following questions regarding listening.

Rate your answer on a 5-point scale according to the following.

How much do you do the following:

	1	2	3	4	5
Item	**Not at all**	**A Little**	**Some-times**	**Frequ ently**	**Almost Always**
1. Look at the person and be attentive to them when you're talking and listening					
2. Put aside what you are doing to show that you are prepared to concentrate on what they are telling you					
3. Ask questions to clarify what they are saying					
4. Repeat back to them what you heard to make sure that you got it right					
5. Feedback to them the feelings that they might be expressing					

6. Ask them for any ideas or solutions that they might have					
7. Summarise at the end of the conversation what you heard and what action will be taken by either of you					
8. If necessary, set a time and date for the next meeting and conversation					

NB: If you really want some powerful feedback, then ask your staff or clients (or even your family!) about each of these items and how well they might see you perform on each one. Maybe get them to fill it out on your behalf.

APPENDIX 2

COMMUNICATION IS MORE ABOUT WHAT YOU DO THAN WHAT YOU SAY

How do others see you? Ask a range of people to rate you on a 1 to 10 rating scale on how they see you. It is of course, an arbitrary scale, but it is still a good guide.

Perhaps you could tell your staff or your clients that you are doing a Communications Course (or similar) and that part of the course is to elicit direct feedback from those around you. People are generally only too happy to assist and it also shows that you are taking yourself seriously and how you communicate with others is important to you.

1. **How approachable do you see me to be   –
   on a scale of 1 to 10
   where 1 is very poor and 10
   is excellent or outstanding?**

Score =

(If the score is not a 9 or a 10 [note that it is rarely ever 10], and the rating falls between a 1 to a 7, then ask, "What would you think that I'd need to do to lift it to an 8 or 9?")

....

....

....

2. How easy am I to relate to –
on a scale of 1 to 10 where
1 is very poor and 10 is
excellent or outstanding?

Score =

(If the score is not a 9 or a 10 [note that it is rarely ever 10], and the rating falls between a 1 to a 7, then ask, "What would you think that I'd need to do to lift it to an 8 or 9?")

....

....

....

....

3. How effective am I as a communicator--
on a scale of 1 to 10 where
1 is very poor and 10 is
excellent or outstanding?

Score =

(If the score is not a 9 or a 10 [note that it is rarely ever 10], and the rating falls between a 1 to a 7, then ask, "What would you think that I'd need to do to lift it to an 8 or 9?")

....

....

....

4. **How would you rate my non-verbal body language in terms of being positive or negative -- where 1 is very poor and 10 is excellent or outstanding?**

Score =

(If the score is not a 9 or a 10 [note that it is rarely ever 10], and the rating falls between a 1 to a 7, then ask, "What would you think that I'd need to do to lift it to an 8 or 9?")

....

....

....

....

APPENDIX 3
COMMUNICATION IS MORE ABOUT WHAT YOU DO THAN WHAT YOU SAY
VERBAL

What do people tell me about what they **like** about **what** I have to say?
(eg. considered, thoughtful, wise, have positive things to say)

....
....
....
....
....
....
....
....
....
....
....

What do people tell me about what they **don't like** about **what** I have to say?
(eg. ill-considered, talks without thinking, frequently negative)

....
....
....
....
....
....
....
....
....
....
....

APPENDIX 3 Continued
NON-VERBAL

What do people tell me about what they **like** about **how** I come across?
(eg. smile often, friendly, good eye contact,

....
....
....
....
....
....
....
....
....
....
....
....

What do people tell me about what they **don't like** about **how** I come across?
(eg. frown, expressionless, look down frequently, funny mannerism)

....
....
....
....
....
....
....
....
....
....
....

MY VISUAL PROMPT

Write down what you will use to prompt you in order for you to be aware of your non-verbals.

Remember, the way the message is sent out affects the way the message is received and it's not what you intended to say or meant to say that counts, it's the way that the other person actually perceives it and takes it on board that counts.

To help me remember, I will use ....

....

....

....

....

....

When will I get it and start to use it ....

....

....

....

....

PARAPHRASE EXERCISES

Paraphrasing is feeding back to the other person what you just heard them tell you. It is about giving back the content of what you heard rather than the emotion or feeling of what you heard.

1. "I'm just not feeling on top of my job at the moment. In fact, I feel pretty darn frustrated and annoyed. Since Jeff was fired from the company for fraudulent activity, I've had to pick up on all his work and now I'm behind on my own. It just doesn't seem fair. Why should I be penalised when I was the one who didn't do anything wrong. I mean, I've been a good worker in this accounts section and worked hard, and now I'm swamped with work and drowning in it, and it's not my fault. It just doesn't seem right. I'm pretty upset about it all."

Your paraphrase:

....

....

....

....

....

....

....

2. "When I joined this company, I thought that there would be some good promotional opportunities. It's one of the things that attracted me here. I mean, it's been 15 months now since I first arrived, and I haven't yet had my first performance appraisal. My boss doesn't give any feedback about how I'm doing. I've really got no idea how I'm going. I'm not sure that he really cares. He seems so caught up in his own work and you'd have to say, he's not the most approachable guy I've ever met. It's just really disappointing. I feel really de-motivated. What do you think that I should do?"

Your paraphrase:

....

....

....

....

....

....

....

3. "Well, I guess you're right. I was kind of hoping that it
wouldn't be obvious that my work isn't up to
scratch....you see, my wife and I are currently separated
and I'm living at my best mate's house...he's got a spare
room. It's not the best, but it's better than nothing...I could
be out on the street you know. It's just really depressing.
I'm just not coping. I know I've been difficult to live with
and she'd just had enough. I guess I don't blame her in a
way. But hell, I really miss her now....and I'm not sure
that she wants me back. I also heard that she was seeing
an old mate of mine. I'm at my wits end....I know my work
has dropped off...I just don't know what to do...how am I
going to get through this?...."

Your paraphrase:

....

....

....

....

....

....

....

APPENDIX 6

PARAPHRASE RESPONSES

Paraphrasing is feeding back to the other person what you just heard them tell you. It is about giving back the **content** of what you heard rather than the **emotion or feeling** of what you heard.

---

1. "I'm just not feeling on top of my job at the moment. In fact, I feel pretty darn frustrated and annoyed. Since Jeff was fired from the company for fraudulent activity, I've had to pick up on all his work and now I'm behind on my own. It just doesn't seem fair. Why should I be penalised when I was the one who didn't do anything wrong. I mean, I've been a good worker in this accounts section and worked hard, and now I'm swamped with work and drowning in it, and it's not my fault. It just doesn't seem right. I'm pretty upset about it all."

Sample Response

1.1 *"You're feeling overwhelmed at the moment because you're totally swamped with work and really through no fault of your own."*

1.2 *"You're a good solid worker who works hard and you like to keep up with your work in accounts, but now, because of someone else's bad behaviour, you're really up against it and struggling with the load put onto you."*

---

2. "When I joined this company, I thought that there would be some good promotional opportunities. It's one of the things that attracted me here. I mean, it's been 15 months now since I first arrived, and I haven't yet had my first performance appraisal. My boss doesn't give any feedback about how I'm doing. I've really got no idea how I'm going. I'm not sure that he really cares. He seems so caught up in his own work and you'd have to say, he's not the most approachable guy I've ever met. It's just really disappointing. I feel really de-motivated. What do you think that I should do?"

Sample Response

2.1 *"You were expecting that you would have had the opportunity for promotion in this organisation, but not only haven't you had your 12 month appraisal, it seems that your boss hasn't given you any feedback of any kind."*

2.2 *"One of the main aspects that attracted you to this job was the opportunity for possible promotion, but it seems that that hasn't happened, but more to the point, your boss doesn't seem to care and further, you haven't even had your first 12 months appraisal."*

---

3. "Well, I guess you're right. I was kind of hoping that it wouldn't be obvious....you see, my wife and I are currently separated and I'm living at my best mate's house...he's got a spare room. It's not the best, but it's better than nothing...I could be out on the street you know. It's just really depressing. I'm just not coping. I know I've been difficult to live with and she'd just had enough. I guess I don't blame her in a way. But hell, I really miss her now....and I'm not sure that she wants me back. I also heard that she was seeing an old mate of mine. I'm at my wits end....I know my work has dropped off...I just don't know what to do...how am I going to get through this...."

Sample Response

3.1 *"What you're saying is that your work has dropped off because of the current drama or relationship breakdown with your wife."*

3.2 *"Because of the current turmoil in your private or personal life, you're not coping well at work here and you're really unsure about what to do or which way to proceed at this point."*

APPENDIX 7

REFLECTION OF FEELING EXERCISES

Reflection of Feeling involves being alert to and responding to the **feeling** being expressed, rather than attending solely to the **content** of what the person says.

It is the ability to be with the person emotionally. It is therefore a very powerful skill.

What the other person is saying is the *content* portion of the message being communicated, but one must also listen to **how** the person says what he or she does.

1. "I'm just kind of confused at the moment. I really don't know what's going on for me. I took this job knowing that there were a few issues to sort out, but I guess that I didn't realise the kind of mess that it was really in. I've tried to get on top of it all, but it's probably true to say that it needed another 3 staff as well to make any headway. I'm just not myself at this point. I've worked hard, very hard over the last 12 months and now, my boss is saying that I've lost my humour and my wife says that I'm grumpy and down. I kind of feel disconnected from my wife and kids. I just don't know....."

Your reflection of feeling:

....

....

....

....

....

....

....

....

....

....

....

....

....

2. "I really enjoyed setting up my business 4 years ago and we make good profit. My wife and I bought it and I trained her up to be the office manager and she really runs it all now. She enjoys her job and I'm glad about that. As for me, I'm kind of lost at this point. I don't enjoy my work any more. There's nothing for me to do. I go to work, open the mail, and then play games on the computer."

Your reflection of feeling:

....

....

....

....

....

....

....

....

....

....

....

3. "I've just been told that I've been sacked. The nice term is "re-trenched". I couldn't really believe it since just 3 weeks previously, they told me that I was performing well as a manager and that in the new re-structure, they would like me to stay on in the new role. I just spent the weekend crying. My husband has tried to console me. I just don't know what to do now."

Your reflection of feeling:

....

....

....

....

....

....

....

....

....

....

....

....

APPENDIX 8

REFLECTION OF FEELING RESPONSES

Reflection of Feeling involves being alert to and responding to the **feeling** being expressed, rather than attending solely to the **content** of what the person says.

---

1. "I'm just kind of confused at the moment. I really don't know what's going on for me. I took this job knowing that there were a few issues to sort out, but I guess that I didn't realise the kind of mess that it was really in. I've tried to get on top of it all, but it's probably true to say that it needed another 3 staff as well to make any headway. I'm just not myself at this point. I've worked hard, very hard over the last 12 months and now, my boss is saying that I've lost my humour and my wife says that I'm grumpy and down. I kind of feel disconnected from my wife and kids. I just don't know....."

Sample Response

1.1 *"You're feeling overwhelmed at this time. You knew that there were some issues in the job initially and you've put in the hard yards for the last 12 months, but now you see that it's actually in a huge mess...enough to really get on top of you and make you feel quite down and maybe even depressed."*

1.2 *"This job has kind of turned you upside down. You knew there were some things to sort out in it, but now you realise what a mess it really is...so you worked hard to fix it all, but it's bigger than you...and now it's kind of burned you out where you're grumpy and disconnected from your* *family…a confusing place to be…one you haven't been in before."*

---

2. "I really enjoyed setting up my business 4 years ago and we make good profit. My wife and I bought it and I trained her up to be the office manager and she really runs it all now. She enjoys her job and I'm glad about that. As for me, I'm kind of lost at this point. I don't enjoy my work any more. There's nothing for me to do. I go to work, open the mail, and then play games on the computer."

Sample Response

2.1 *"Well done on setting up your business, making profit and getting your wife involved. However, having done all that, you've nothing left to do, and as a result are feeling lost."*

2.2 *"You've obviously done well to set up a profitable business and to also allow your wife to be involved which she enjoys. The business is running well, but now there's little if anything for you to do. You're lost. Maybe lost your purpose and not feeling fulfilled at all."*

---

3. "I've just been told that I've been sacked. The nice term is "re-trenched." I couldn't really believe it since just 3 weeks previously, they told me that I was performing well as a manager and that in the new re-structure, they would like me to stay on in the new role. I just spent the weekend crying. My husband has tried to console me. I just don't know what to do now."

Sample Response

3.1 *"You're in a state of shock. You can't believe that you've been sacked after all the positives that you'd recently received. It's devastated you and now you're at a loss as to what to do."*

3.2 *"You can't believe it. After all the positive feedback that you've been receiving to now be suddenly sacked. Seems incomprehensible. Not only has it devastated you, but it has left you completely up in the air about what to do now."*

ABOUT THE AUTHOR

**Dr Darryl Cross
(PhD)**
**Leadership Coach &
Psychologist**

- *Fellow, Australian Psychological Society*
- *Fellow, Australian Institute of Management*
- *Graduate, Australian Institute of Company Directors*
- *Certified Personal & Executive Coach, College of Executive Coaching*
- *Certified Mentor Coach, College of Executive Coaching*
- *Member, International Coach Federation*
- *Accredited Facilitator, Mindshop Australia Ltd*
- *Accredited Advisor, Family Business Association*
- *Foreign Affiliate, American Psychological Association*

Darryl is a clinical and organisational psychologist as well as an internationally accredited professional certified coach. He is an author, international speaker and university lecturer.

Darryl assists people to maximize their potential and reach their goals.

- For **executives and senior managers**, this might mean a focus on effective leadership, dealing with difficult staff, increasing productivity and succession planning.
- For those with **business concerns**, it might mean work-life balance, career progression, job dissatisfaction or dealing with conflict.
- For those with **personal concerns**, it may include lack of direction, lack of confidence or relational issues.

He has coached clients from the ABN Group, MediCare Australia, DSTO, ZF Lemforder Pty Ltd, Catholic Education, SAGE Automation, SA Housing Trust, DIMIA, Philmac Pty Ltd, and Schiavello Pty Ltd to name a few. His clients are at various global points including, England, Dubai, Ireland and Canada.

Academic training in psychology and specific training in coaching together with life experience, means that Darryl has come up with practical ways to use life principles that work. He has the knack of being able to say it all simply.

Having gone through the discipline of tertiary study, he completed his Psychology Honours Degree in Psychology at Flinders University in South Australia. He gained his Doctorate in Psychology from the University of Queensland.

As a **Leadership Coach**, Darryl has completed a Professional Development Certificate in Coaching Practice through the Department of Psychology at the University of Sydney. Later, he completed graduate studies in coaching with the College of Executive Coaching (CEC) in California, USA. He qualified to be a Professional Certified Coach with the International Coach Federation. More recently, he completed the course to be a Mentor Coach with the CEC.

He **knows how organisations work** from his first appointment for three years as an Occupational Psychologist with the Federal Government and then when he was also appointed as a Director of a unit at the Adelaide Children's Hospital and held that position until moving into his own business in the late 1980's. He has acted as a **management consultant** to a range of companies and government departments and has conducted attitude and stress surveys and 360 assessments for leaders as well as assist in developing positive culture in organisations.

As a **University Lecturer**, he has tutored and lectured in Psychology at the University of Queensland in Brisbane for seven years and lectured in the Masters Programs in Psychology at Macquarie University in Sydney, New South Wales for two years. He formerly was a sessional Lecturer in "Leadership Dynamics" for the MBA Program in the International Graduate School of Business at the

University of South Australia as well as a similar program at Torrens University.

Darryl Cross has been **speaking and training** for over three decades on a variety of keynotes and workshops for business, professional and non-professional groups on topics ranging from "Stress Management", "Coping with Change", "Handling the Angry Customer", "Career Progression" to "Management Styles". More recently, he has run a coaching program training executive and managers with the ABN Group in both Perth and Melbourne.

As an **author**, Darryl has published numerous papers for national and overseas academic journals, as well as for the popular press. He has written books on raising adolescents, parenting, stopping self-sabotage, depression at work and how to pursue success and happiness. He has also authored a career guidance test called the *"Vocational Interest Questionnaire"* which is available on-line for both adolescents and adults.

He is heard regularly on talk-back radio in Adelaide and nationally and is often seen on various segments on Adelaide television as well as in the print media. He knows what he's talking about and is called upon to give his opinion.

He understands human behaviour and therefore can help individuals and teams to move to another place.

www.DrDarryl.com

www.LeadershipCoaching.com.au

www.FindACareerPath.com

www.MyFutureCareer.com.au

www.TeenagerTroubleShooting.com

www.GrowingUpChildren.com

www.HowToStopSelfSabotage.com

www.DepressionAtWork.com

www.SuccessPursuit.com

www.ListenUpNow.com.au

www.ingramcontent.com/pod-product-compliance
Lightning Source LLC
Chambersburg PA
CBHW071209200326
41519CB00018B/5437